Library of Congress Cataloging-in-Publication Data

Watts, Barrie.
    Butterfly and caterpillar.

    (Stopwatch books)
    Includes index.
    Summary: Photographs follow the development of a
butterfly from mating to birth of the caterpillar to
chrysalis to the emergence of the butterfly.
    I. Pierris brassicae—Juvenile literature.
2. Butterflies—Juvenile literature. 3. Caterpillars—
Juvenile literature. [I. Butterflies. 2. Caterpillars.
3. Metamorphosis] I. Title. II. Series.
QL561.P5W38 1986   595.78'9043   86-10050
ISBN 0-382-09291-0
ISBN 0-382-09282-I (lib. bdg.)

First published by A & C Black (Publishers) Limited
35 Bedford Row, London WC1R 4JH

© 1985 Barrie Watts

Published in the United States in 1986
by Silver Burdett Company
Morristown, New Jersey

Acknowledgements
The artwork is by B L Kearley Ltd.

Butterfly
and caterpillar

Barrie Watts

Stopwatch books

 Silver Burdett Company • Morristown, New Jersey

Here is a butterfly.

Have you ever seen a butterfly like this one?
It is called a cabbage white butterfly and it lives
in parks and gardens.

There are many different kinds of butterflies.
They all start life as tiny eggs like these.

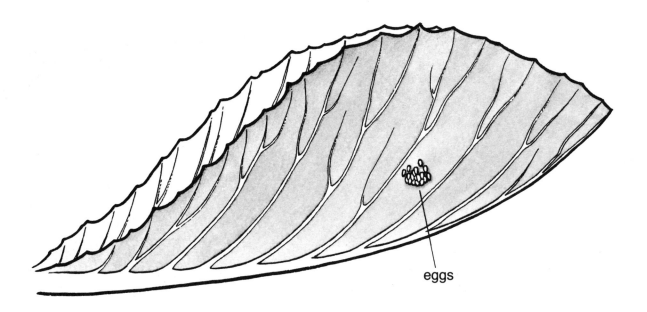

eggs

This book will tell you how a butterfly comes from an egg.

Here are a male butterfly and a female butterfly.

Look at these two butterflies.

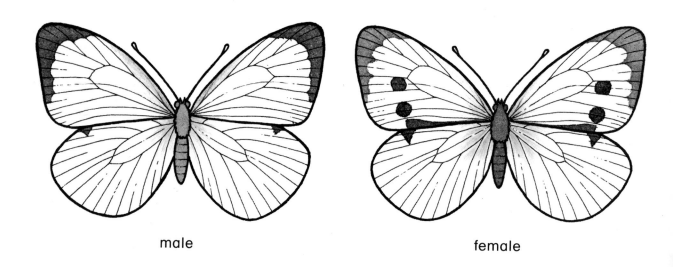

male

female

Can you see that each butterfly has two pairs of wings?
The female butterfly has black spots on her front wings.
The male does not have spots on his front wings.

Now look at the photograph. The male butterfly and
the female butterfly are mating. They stay like this
for about two hours. Then the male flies away and the
female is ready to lay her eggs.

The butterfly lays her eggs.

The butterfly looks for the right place to lay her eggs.

Look at this picture.

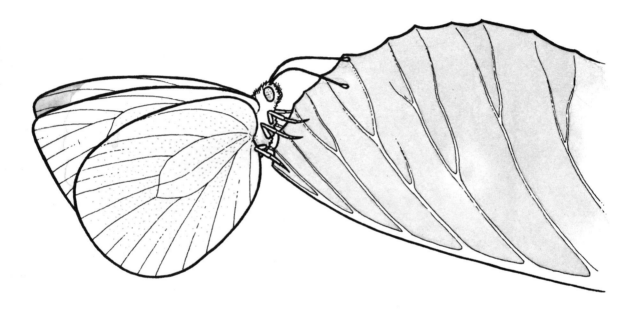

Can you see the long antennae on the butterfly's head?
The butterfly uses her antennae to smell each plant.
She will lay her eggs on a cabbage leaf.

Now look at the photograph. The butterfly sticks each
yellow egg underneath a leaf. After she has laid her
eggs, the butterfly will die.

6

Caterpillars come out of the eggs.

Here are the butterfly's eggs.

This photograph shows the eggs very large.
In real life, the eggs are about the size of a pin head.

Inside each egg, a caterpillar is beginning to grow.
After ten days the eggs are ready to hatch.
Look at the big photograph. Each caterpillar eats a hole
in its egg shell and wriggles out. The caterpillars
are very hungry. They eat the empty egg shells.

The caterpillars grow very fast.

Now the caterpillars start to eat the cabbage plant.
They only like to eat cabbage. Look at the photograph.
This caterpillar is using its strong jaws to munch through
a leaf. It eats all the time and grows very quickly.

As the caterpillar grows, its skin gets too tight.
Soon the caterpillar's skin begins to split, like this.

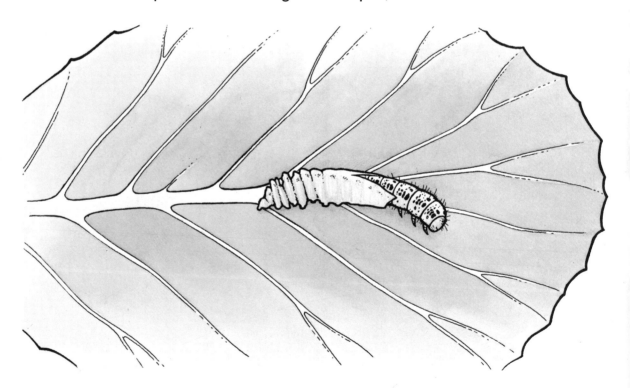

The caterpillar has a new skin underneath. It will change
skins four times before it is fully grown.

The caterpillar is fully grown.

After three weeks, the caterpillar is fully grown.
Look at the photograph. The caterpillar has a hairy
body. It is divided into thirteen segments.

Here is a drawing of a caterpillar.

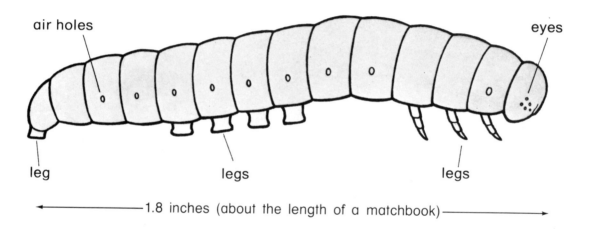

air holes

eyes

leg

legs

legs

1.8 inches (about the length of a matchbook)

The caterpillar's eyes are small, so it cannot see
very well. It breathes through air holes on the side
of its body. Look at the caterpillar's legs. It uses
its legs and feet to grip onto the leaf.

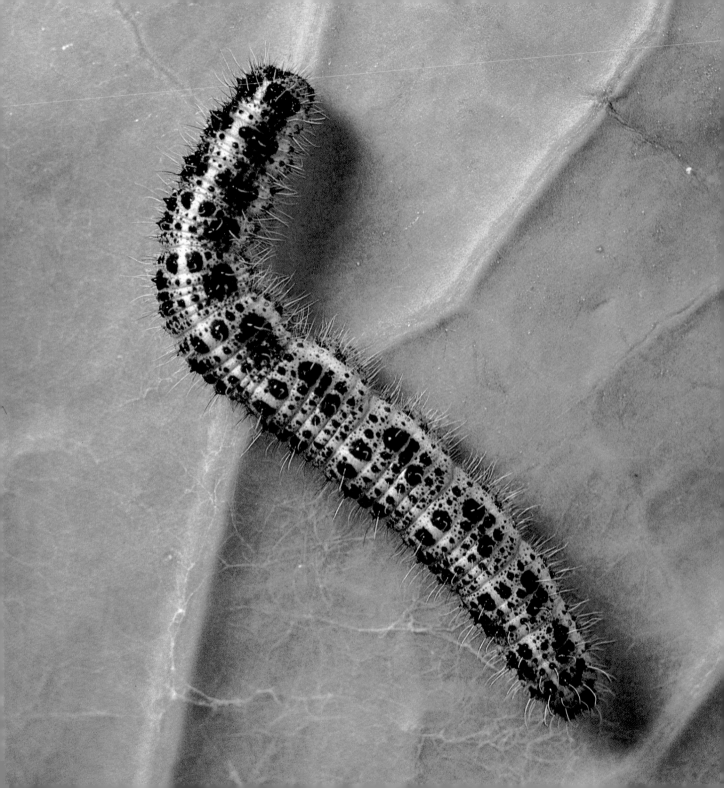

The caterpillar finds a place to rest.

The caterpillar stops eating. It crawls away from the cabbage plant and finds a safe place to rest.

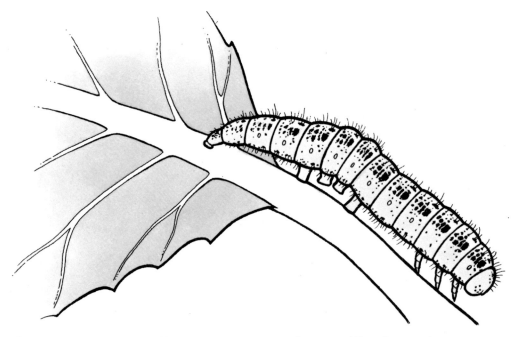

Soon the caterpillar starts to spin a silk thread. The thread comes out of a hole which is just below the caterpillar's mouth.

Look at the photograph. This caterpillar is resting on a garden fence. It makes a pad of silk thread to lie on. Then it spins a silk thread around its body. This thread holds the caterpillar onto the fence.

The caterpillar turns into a chrysalis.

Soon the caterpillar's skin begins to split, like this.

Can you see the old skin coming off and the shiny green case underneath? The caterpillar has turned into a chrysalis.

Look at the big photograph. The new chrysalis is soft but in a few hours it will harden. Can you see the thin silk thread on the chrysalis? This will keep the chrysalis from falling off its silk pad.

A butterfly comes out of the chrysalis.

The chrysalis stays on its silk pad for weeks or even months. Inside the chrysalis, a butterfly is growing.

Can you see the spots on the butterfly's wing inside this chrysalis? The butterfly is ready to come out.

The butterfly pushes from inside until the case splits open. Then it slowly struggles out of the case. Its wings are soft and crumpled like a damp cloth.

The butterfly dries its wings.

The butterfly is very tired. It rests on the empty chrysalis. Slowly its wings unfold.

After about an hour, the butterfly's wings are the right shape. But they are still damp and soft. The butterfly will have to wait for about two hours before its wings are dry. Then it will be ready to fly.

The butterfly gets food from flowers.

Flowers make a sugary liquid called nectar.
The butterfly uses its long hollow tongue to suck up
the nectar. It's sort of like drinking through a straw.

Look at the photograph. Can you see the butterfly's
tongue poking into the flower? When the butterfly
is not feeding its tongue is kept curled up.

Soon the female butterfly will mate and lay some
eggs, like this.

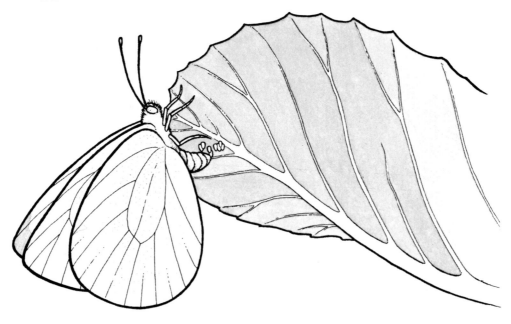

What do you think will happen to the eggs?

Do you remember how the butterfly came from the egg?
See if you can tell the story in your own words.
You can use these pictures to help you.

1

2

4

5

Index

This index will help you to find some of the important words in the book

3

6

To watch a caterpillar grow, keep one in a large jar. Cover it with a lid which has small holes in. Put tissue in the bottom and cabbage for the caterpillar to eat. Make sure you change the tissue and food every day.